Gender Identity

By Anika Abraham

Cavendish
Square

New York

Published in 2022 by Cavendish Square Publishing, LLC
29 E. 21st Street New York, NY 10010

Website: cavendishsq.com

This publication represents the opinions and views of the author based on his or her personal
experience, knowledge, and research. The information in this book serves as a general guide
only. The author and publisher have used their best efforts in preparing this book and disclaim
liability rising directly or indirectly from the use and application of
this book.

Portions of this work were originally authored by Charlie Light and published as *Gender
Identity: The Search for Self* (*Hot Topics*). All new material this edition authored by
Anika Abraham.

All websites were available and accurate when this book was sent to press.

Library of Congress Cataloging-in-Publication Data

Names: Abraham, Anika, author.
Title: Gender identity / by Anika Abraham.
Description: First edition. | New York : Cavendish Square Publishing,
[2022] | Series: Topics today | Includes bibliographical references and
index.
Identifiers: LCCN 2020014414 (print) | LCCN 2020014415 (ebook) | ISBN
9781502660930 (library binding) | ISBN 9781502660923 (paperback) | ISBN
9781502660947 (ebook)
Subjects: LCSH: Gender identity–Juvenile literature. | Gender
nonconformity–Juvenile literature.
Classification: LCC HQ18.55 .A27 2022 (print) | LCC HQ18.55 (ebook) | DDC
305.3–dc23
LC record available at https://lccn.loc.gov/2020014414
LC ebook record available at https://lccn.loc.gov/2020014415

Editor: Katie Kawa
Copyeditor: Nicole Horning
Designer: Deanna Paternostro

Some of the images in this book illustrate individuals who are models. The depictions do not
imply actual situations or events.

CPSIA compliance information: Batch #CS22CSQ: For further information contact Cavendish Square Publishing LLC, New York,
New York, at 1-877-980-4450.

Printed in the United States of America

Find us on

CONTENTS

A PLACE
IN HISTORY

Throughout history, people from marginalized and oppressed communities have seldom been given a voice or been able to tell their stories from their own perspectives. Too often, some groups have been the subject of ridicule and discrimination, pushed to the edges of society and shunned.

Some of these oppressed and misunderstood communities have included those identifying as transgender, nonbinary, gender nonconforming, and intersex. These people have always existed; however, their stories were often unheard. Through the years, many people have grappled with their gender identity, trying to fit in a world filled with little compassion for those who don't fit into stereotypical gender roles. Many have bravely lived as their authentic selves, but many others have faced harsh treatment and have lived in great fear because of who they are or who they love—sometimes even having to hide their true identity to protect themselves or feel accepted. This has often been the case for many members of the LGBTQ+ community. LGBTQ+ stands for lesbian, gay, bisexual, transgender, and queer or questioning.

Discussions of gender identity and expression may seem new to some, but they have their roots far back in human history. In order to gain a well-rounded perspective on this

◀ Members of the LGBTQ+ community have fought throughout history for rights and acceptance.

topic, it's important to look at the history of the LGBTQ+ community as a whole and how the treatment of members of this community and the understanding of the diversity within this community have changed and evolved over time.

Ancient Acceptance

Acceptance of LGBTQ+ individuals in ancient societies, such as Greece and Rome, has been debated by scholars and historians. According to some accounts, these societies may have been places where same-sex relationships were commonplace, and even encouraged. In ancient Sparta, there was an army called the Band of Lovers that same-sex couples would join. The island of Lesbos is known for the ancient Greek poet Sappho, whose work has been interpreted by

LGBTQ+ individuals have existed throughout history, including in ancient Greece.

some as descriptions of love and desire between women, although little is known for sure about her personal life and the actual meaning of her poems. Still, Lesbos gave rise to the term "lesbianism," or romantic or sexual relationships between two women.

Ages of Improvement

Relationships between same-sex couples, as well as stories about people whose gender expression—the outward expression of their gender identity—didn't fit the traditional norms of their time, have been known throughout the ages, but these stories were often hidden from so-called polite society. In the 19th and 20th centuries, people such as Dr. Mary Edwards Walker, the American Civil War's only female surgeon and the only woman to earn the Medal of Honor, and singer Gladys Bentley—both of whom preferred to dress in clothing generally reserved for men—were considered controversial but respected for their talents. By the 1920s, different ideas about gender were coming more into the forefront, pushed in ways that challenged tradition through the introduction of different hairstyles, more modern clothing styles, and more demands for equality.

As the decades passed, however, society became stricter and less adventurous. In the United States, the typical nuclear family hinged on traditional gender roles: The man was often the main provider,

Mary Edwards Walker was known for dressing in men's clothing. She was a leading voice for dress reform during her time.

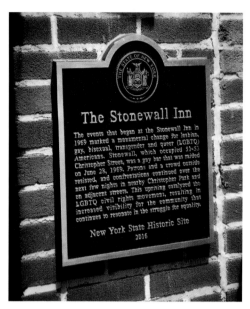

As noted on this plaque, the Stonewall riots of 1969 were the start of huge changes for the LGBTQ+ community and its pursuit of civil rights.

while the woman stayed at home taking care of children. Still, there were some people who defied societal expectations of sexuality and gender. These people, however, were often prohibited from expressing themselves in public. If they did, they risked fines or jail time.

Then, in 1969, members of the LGBTQ+ community took part in an uprising that led to many changes. The name of the Stonewall riots (or simply "Stonewall") became a rallying cry for LGBTQ+ rights throughout the United States. On June 28, 1969, police raided a nightclub called the Stonewall Inn in New York City. The club was a place where young gay, lesbian, and transgender people gathered to socialize and be themselves without harassment from the public. However, police harassment was common. On the night the Stonewall riots started, the police entered the club, targeting and harassing patrons. They arrested a number of people as well. Similar raids had been happening for quite some time, but this time, people fought back. They took to the streets in protest, hurling objects at police and voicing their outrage. The uprising took place, on and off, for five days and brought people together in protest. This event is often seen as the foundation of the modern LGBTQ+ movement. Today, the Stonewall Inn is a national monument.

Throughout the 1970s and 1980s, the LGBTQ+ community worked for more advances toward acceptance and equality, and more people began to openly identify as members of this community. Then, the HIV/AIDS epidemic erupted in the late 1980s. Because many people associated AIDS with gay men because they were the group most brutally affected at the time (although anyone can get this disease through the transfer of bodily fluids from an infected person), this created a stigma around the LGBTQ+ community and further devastated the community with thousands of deaths.

In the 1990s and early 2000s, however, things slowly changed as more people expressed their true identities and fought for acceptance in their families, social circles, and the world at large. Members of the LGBTQ+ community began to push even more for equal rights, including the right to safely and openly express and identify their gender on their terms.

Around the world, LGBTQ+ advocates are standing up for equal rights.

Today's View

In the 21st century, people have made a number of advances in the fight for LGBTQ+ rights. People who are transgender, nonbinary, gender nonconforming, and intersex have struggled for rights and acceptance but have made important progress. Historical milestones such as the women's and civil rights movements of the 1960s and 1970s, along with more recent movements toward human rights for all, have played a large role in opening people's minds. Now, more young people and even older adults are coming out and sharing their true selves with others in a number of different ways. However, there's still a long road to travel in terms of increasing awareness and acceptance.

In recent years, some people have felt empowered to push back against progressive social standards around the United States and, to some extent, the world. Increased instances of prejudice are once more grabbing international and local headlines. One example is in state and local governments around the country, where politicians have introduced bills that target transgender youth and others.

According to a *USA Today* article discussing results from a 2018 poll that tracked LGBTQ+ acceptance trends, "Young people are growing less tolerant of LGBTQ individuals, a jarring turn for a generation traditionally considered embracing and open."[1] Nevertheless, there is hope that the future will be brighter for LGBTQ+ individuals. Instances of progress and acceptance are becoming more common, as younger generations stand up for social issues they care about and more liberal politicians garner support from all areas of society. Industries such as book publishing and media such as television and films are also producing more supportive works and series focused on the LGBTQ+ community, encouraging empathy and kindness toward all people.

Intentions

This book aims to help readers understand gender identity. It takes readers on a journey through definitions of gender identity now and in the past, highlighting key moments, figures, and statistics relating to gender identity and LGBTQ+ communities. Ultimately, this book

Similar Terms, Different Meanings

Some terms related to gender identity may sound similar to each other. However, they have different meanings. This guide considers four terms and their definitions to better help you understand and navigate terminology in this book.

Term	Definition
gender identity	How a person sees and thinks of their own gender; this can be male, female, a combination of both, or neither.
gender expression	The way a person uses how they look and act to show their gender identity.
gender dysphoria	Distress caused by the sex (and, typically, gender) a person is assigned at birth not matching their gender identity. This may lead someone to transition, or work to match their gender expression with their gender identity.
transgender	Relating to a person whose gender identity does not match the sex they were assigned at birth.

These are some of the terms related to gender identity that will be found throughout this book. Language is always changing and means different things to different people. Therefore, language that is not considered offensive today or to certain people may be considered offensive in the future or to a different individual. It's important to listen respectfully and change your words accordingly if someone asks you not to use a certain word, term, or pronoun because it offends them.

seeks to promote acceptance of all people and make readers better educated and aware of the many diverse forms of gender expression and identity in this world, shaping readers into more active, attuned, and conscientious global citizens. It also provides information on organizations working hard daily for those identifying as transgender, nonbinary, gender nonconforming, and intersex. If you feel like you are in need of such services, or if you want to know more about gender identity, resource information is also available at the back of this book.

UNDERSTANDING SEX

Sex and gender are concepts closely related to understanding one's gender identity. For a long time, people thought these words were interchangeable. However, sex and gender are distinct things with varying definitions. To understand them best, we must look at them individually and through the lens of history.

Only Male and Female?

For a long time, many people assumed that humans were divided only into female and male categories. This understanding still exists today and is called the gender binary (binary meaning "two"). They also assumed that all infants were born with anatomy that was considered either entirely female or entirely male and that an infant's anatomy determines how they choose to express themselves throughout their lifetime. In believing this, they assumed that sex and gender mean the same thing.

Society's ideas about gender are rooted in its traditional ideas about anatomy, namely that human bodies come in only two forms: female and male. The gender binary builds on this belief by outlining which behaviors and appearances are considered feminine and which are masculine.

◀ Sex is assigned to someone at birth based on anatomical features.

In reality, sex and gender are both far more complex than society often acknowledges.

From Birth

Doctors assign a sex to an infant at birth, generally based only on the appearance of the baby's genitals. Infants with vaginas are designated female, and infants with penises are designated male. Some

A baby's assigned sex at birth might not match their gender identity later in life.

medical and scientific organizations refer to the category associated with a person's genitals as their "biological sex." However, some people find this term offensive because it oversimplifies the complexities of sex and gender. "Assigned sex" or "designated sex" are largely considered more appropriate, but it is a matter of individual choice. This book will use "assigned sex" to refer to the sex an infant is designated at birth.

People often confuse sex and gender because society links them so closely together. However, they refer to different aspects of a person's identity, and the terms cannot be used interchangeably. A person's assigned sex is a label given based on their anatomy. Assigned gender is often based on assigned sex and refers to how a person is perceived and treated by their family, friends, and society. This is because the gender binary operates on the belief that anatomy determines many aspects of human personalities, abilities, interests, and identities. However, human anatomy is much more complex than this binary acknowledges. When you take a closer look at sex and its many variations, it becomes evident how society has artificially created the link between sex and gender.

Characteristics of Puberty

Sex is actually defined by four primary characteristics and many secondary characteristics that develop during puberty. This is a time when many biological and psychological transformations happen within the human body. Many emotions come into play as well, and young people may consider their gender identity or come to accept it.

Puberty can be a tricky time of life to navigate. People typically experience increased levels of estrogen and testosterone or increased levels of one hormone or the other in their bodies. Changes in hormones result in the development of certain traits, such as facial hair, breasts, wider hips, an Adam's apple, or a lowered voice. These are all secondary sex characteristics. Society designates certain secondary sex characteristics as female, such as breasts, and others as male, such as facial hair.

Puberty comes with many physical changes and can also be a time when people consider their gender identity.

Primary sex characteristics include genitals (external), sex organs (internal), hormones (secreted by glands), and chromosomes (part of a person's DNA). Human beings typically have 46 chromosomes, which are grouped into 23 pairs. Scientists refer to the 23rd pair as sex chromosomes, and they generally come in two forms: X and Y. Most people are born with either XX chromosomes or XY chromosomes. These pairs are associated with different traits. The majority of people with XX chromosomes are born with and later develop sex traits that society considers female, while the majority of people with XY chromosomes are born with and develop sex traits that society considers male. One of the most common misconceptions is that a person's sex chromosomes always match their other sex characteristics, which is not always true. A person can have sex chromosomes typically associated with males but secondary (or even other primary) sex characteristics associated with females.

Menstruation and Physical Changes

Most people with anatomy that society considers female experience puberty between the ages of 7 and 19. When they enter puberty, they will generally begin to experience a menstrual cycle, more commonly known as a period. This process is essentially a person's body preparing for pregnancy. Most people who are assigned female are capable of becoming pregnant after puberty.

As a person enters the menstrual cycle, their reproductive system begins to produce egg cells called ova or oocytes. The average cycle occurs over 28 days and consists of three phases: follicular, ovulatory, and luteal. If these eggs are fertilized with sperm during the ovulation phase, the person may become pregnant. In the luteal phase, if they have not become pregnant, the lining of the uterus sheds and leaves the body (menstruation).

During puberty, people with anatomy society considers female typically experience other physical changes as well. For instance, their hips begin to widen, and they develop breasts, which vary in size from person to person. Hair begins to grow in their armpits, on their legs, and in their pubic region.

Changes for Others

People with anatomy society considers male typically experience different changes during puberty. The testicles grow bigger, followed by the penis. The scrotum darkens, grows, hangs down, and develops hair follicles. Pubic hair begins to grow on the scrotum and above the penis and often spreads over time. Generally, a person with a penis becomes able to ejaculate about a year after their testicles begin to grow. At this point, they are capable of reproduction. Vocal changes generally occur during this time as well. Their voice will lower over time and will often crack during the process.

Shared Changes

While these are the typical changes during puberty, everyone develops at their own rate, and there are many variances in these developments. Often, people will experience changes that society does not typically associate with their assigned sex. For example, many people who are assigned male will also experience some level of breast development. The American Academy of Pediatrics (AAP) explained, "Early in puberty, most boys experience soreness or tenderness around their nipples. Three in four, if not more, will actually have some breast growth, the result of a biochemical reaction that converts some of their testosterone to the female sex hormone, estrogen."[1] Rather than following a strict binary, primary and secondary sex characteristics have a wide variety of possibilities.

Traits and Conditions of Intersex Individuals

Many people have sexual or reproductive anatomical traits that do not conform to the male/female binary. For example, it is possible for a person to have XX chromosomes and a penis, which is considered male genitalia. Vice versa, a person may have XY chromosomes and a vagina, which is considered the female genitalia. There are a wide variety of these variations, and they are all referred to under the umbrella term "intersex." Another term is "differences or disorders of sex development" (DSD). According to the American Psychological Association, "[Experts] feel this term is more accurate and less stigmatizing than the term intersex."[2] However, both of these terms can be controversial to different people because the language of how we define ourselves is deeply personal.

Sometimes intersex traits are present at birth, while others don't become apparent until later in life. Still others are not discovered during a person's lifetime. This is one of the many reasons for the misconception that intersex traits are extremely rare. It's currently impossible to know exactly how many intersex infants are born, but

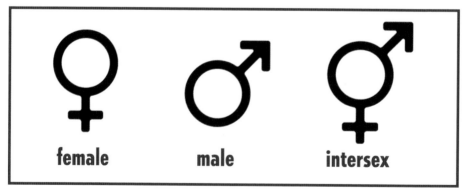

female   male   intersex

A person who is intersex may have male and female characteristics or parts.

A Common "Solution"

No two intersex people are biologically the same—in fact, there are thousands of combinations that could classify someone as intersex—and their personal stories are equally unique. However, many intersex people face common issues. One in particular is that of surgery to change intersex traits. These types of surgeries are sometimes called "gender normalization" surgeries, and they have been taking place since the 1950s. Often, the recipients of the surgery are too young to remember this surgery and their parents or guardians never tell them about it. However, the effects of such surgeries have devastated many.

Even when intersex infants are perfectly healthy, doctors will often perform genital surgery for no reason other than to assign them a sex. The practice of performing medically unnecessary genital surgery reveals the harmful effects of the gender binary. The Intersex Society of North America (ISNA) does recommend that "following diagnostic work-up, newborns with intersex should be given a 'gender assignment' as boy or girl, depending on which of those genders the child is more likely to feel as she or he grows up."[1] However, it does not advocate for surgery. This is because when doctors and parents decide to alter an infant's anatomy simply to give them a sex, the societal pressure to label everyone as either female or male outweighs the rights of the infant and the risks of the surgery. Many intersex people don't know their own medical history because their parents and doctors keep it from them. This practice is deeply troubling to many people as it disrespects the rights of intersex individuals, and the surgeries are often irreversible. Likewise, it forces an individual into a gender category they may not identify with later in life. Today, many intersex people who are aware of having had surgery are speaking out and making their own decisions about their gender.

1. INSA, "Frequently Asked Questions," isna.org/faq/printable (accessed March 16, 2020).

a 2017 report by the Human Rights Watch organization estimated:

> *As many as 1.7 percent of babies are different from what is typically called a boy or a girl. The chromosomes, gonads, internal or external genitalia in these children ... differ from social expectations. Around 1 in 2,000 babies is different enough that doctors may recommend surgical intervention to make the body appear more in line with those expectations.*[3]

This is about the same number of people who have red hair in the United States, so it's not nearly as rare as people might think.

Parental Steps

There are many steps parents can take to ensure their intersex children are healthy, happy, and fulfilled. Some ways recommended by the ISNA include getting informed about intersex identities and issues, consulting a mental health professional such as a psychologist or another counselor, and connecting with the larger intersex community.

Intersex advocacy groups around the world help people who are intersex connect with others who can relate to their experiences. Some examples are the ISNA; interACT, which focuses on

The LGBTQ+ rainbow flag is a symbol of this community and all who are a part of it, including many who are intersex.

intersex youth and young adults; Gender Spectrum; and the Intersex Campaign for Equality. These organizations fight for the rights of intersex children and adults and work to increase public awareness of people who are intersex and the issues they face and to destigmatize intersex traits and conditions.

Backing Off of Binary

The gender binary is something that's been rooted in many people's understandings for far too long. Gender Spectrum, a group promoting gender sensitivity and education for children and teens, explained, "Western culture has come to view gender as a binary concept, with two rigidly fixed options: male or female, both grounded in a person's physical anatomy."[4] This is supported in different ways, including through the media, in books, and in religion—all of which have helped prolong and uphold stereotypes of male and female concepts. Traditionally, society has linked its concept of female anatomy to a female gender and its concept of male anatomy to a male gender. Today, it's important to keep in mind that sex and gender are two different things. A person's assigned sex does not determine their gender.

In reality, there are many different sex characteristics, and having one or more of them does not mean a person has to identify as male or female. If more of society can embrace this reality, more people will be able to express themselves freely, regardless of how they identify.

Your Opinion Matters!

1. What do the words "sex" and "gender" mean to you? Why do you think this way? Did reading this chapter make you think differently than you did before?

2. What does it mean to be intersex? What important issues or concepts do people who are intersex have to consider?

3. How can advocacy groups help different types of people in the world? Do you think they are useful? Why or why not?

UNDERSTANDING GENDER

Gender is at the heart of gender identity, but what is it? That's a question with many answers. In reality, gender encompasses many different things, and therefore it doesn't have one definition. People experience gender in different ways. Every day, people listen to different messages associated with gender. It's up to each person to find the meaning that best fits for them. It's likewise important for each person to understand how gender functions in the wider world and how this understanding can help educate others around them.

Socially Formed

Society has often believed that a person's sex determines many aspects of who they are, such as their appearance, abilities, interests, and behaviors. These aspects—the state of being seen and understood as male, female, a mix of both, or neither—are all lumped under the term "gender." As society often divides sex into a female and male binary, it also divides gender into a female and male binary.

Society determines which behaviors, occupations, skills, interests, and personality traits are "normal" for the female gender and which are "normal" for the male gender. Social norms

◀ The idea of a strict gender binary—male and female—is changing in today's society.

based on a person's gender are called gender roles. Gender roles are not universal—each society has its own variation of gender roles, and some cultures recognize more than two genders. A trait that is considered masculine in one culture may be considered feminine in another and vice versa. These variations demonstrate that gender roles are a social construct, or something that has been invented and promoted by people in a society.

In the simplest of terms, ideas about gender are made up. A person is not born believing that pink is for girls and blue is for boys, that girls are passive and boys are bold, that women are instinctively compassionate and men are logical by nature, or any of the other innumerable stereotypes about what's considered feminine and

Society often dictates the gender binary. Girls might be expected to wear dresses and grow long hair, while boys might be expected to wear pants and have short hair. However, these ideas are changing.

what's considered masculine. Instead, these stereotypes are learned from external sources as a person matures. The actions and attitudes of family, friends, teachers, classmates, and acquaintances are absorbed. These interactions slowly shape a person's understanding of gender as they grow up, generally without them even noticing. Gender is also learned about through other sources: the news, religion, movies, television, social media, music, books, magazines, advertisements, and many others.

When similar messages are observed from multiple sources, a person begins to believe that these messages about gender must be true. This makes it easy to fall into the belief that these "differences" between the female gender and the male gender are natural, instinctual, or even biological.

Gender and Discrimination

Gender roles are more complex—and more harmful—than a clean division between female and male. Society often sees the categories of female and male as competing forces. Rather than treating both women and men equally, many societies have historically given men more social and economic power than women, and in many ways, this continues to be true today. Women have historically been discriminated against based on their gender. While anyone can experience gender-based discrimination, cisgender men (men whose gender identity matches their assigned sex) have historically benefited socially and economically by discriminating against women and transgender people. Although there has been significant progress, discrimination and violence toward women and transgender people are still a big issue today.

Gender is not the only basis for discrimination women experience. Stereotypes based on race, disability, religion, and many other factors can also impact the discrimination and violence many women experience. Racial, religious, ableist, and other prejudices must be acknowledged and combated alongside gender-based discrimination. Objectification, violence, and discrimination—especially at work—are just some of the issues that women face.

Difficulties for Women

In both personal relationships and in forms of media such as advertisements, women are often seen as sexual objects or possessions rather than as people. This behavior values women based on their physical appearance and holds women to unrealistic beauty standards that can lead to low self-esteem and other issues. Treating women this way is both disrespectful and dehumanizing. This is called objectification, and it leads to further discrimination and violence against women.

Other concerning issues for women include sexual and physical violence. Sexual and physical violence against women and abusive behaviors such as stalking continue to be a problem in society. According to the Centers for Disease Control and Prevention (CDC), "More than 1 in 3 women and 1 in 4 men have experienced sexual violence including physical contact at some point in their lives."[1] Many of the cases of sexual and physical violence are committed by people the victims knew. However, some attackers are completely unknown to the victims.

Discrimination in the Workplace

Discrimination against women exists within personal relationships and within social structures such as work environments. One example is the pay gap between women and men. Despite the fact that the Equal Pay Act was passed in 1963, saying that men and women should be paid equally for doing the same job, discrimination still exists in the workforce. According to the American Association of University Women, "On average women in America are paid only 82 cents for every dollar paid to men. At the current rate of progress, the pay gap will not close until 2093."[2] This study also found that women of color are affected even more severely than white women. For example, on average, African American women earn 62 cents on the dollar paid to men, Latinx women earn 54 cents on the dollar, and Native American women earn 57 cents on the dollar. There is some hope that the situation will improve for women all around the United States, however. In March 2019, the House of

Representatives voted to pass an amendment to the Equal Pay Act called the Paycheck Fairness Act. This piece of legislature, if also passed by the Senate, would improve loopholes in the current Equal Pay Act and make the conditions of the act more binding. It would also protect employees from penalties or consequences if they discuss salaries and provide for negotiation training for women and girls, among other things.

Gender roles and stereotypes often affect women negatively at work.

Children and Gender

Children absorb messages about gender at a rapid pace. Around the age of two, most children can distinguish the physical difference between typical female and male anatomy. By three years old, they can identify their own assigned sex. They also already understand which clothes, toys, and activities are considered "normal" for their assigned sex and which are "off-limits." Children quickly learn which of their behaviors and preferences are praised, rewarded, or encouraged because of their assigned sex and which are rejected, mocked, or discouraged. Before a child has celebrated their fifth birthday, they are already beginning to internalize society's messages about gender.

Family and friends often give children toys based on gender roles. Children assigned as girls receive dolls, dollhouses, stuffed animals, and other "feminine" toys, while children assigned as boys receive "masculine" toys such as cars, action figures, and sporting equipment. This separation of genders through toys is reinforced through the media children consume. Commercials often show girls playing with dollhouses and boys playing with vehicles and action figures. Toys are physically separated into boys' and girls' aisles in most stores, and this division is generally marked by color: pink or purple toys for girls and blue, green, red, and orange for boys. All of these factors send children (and adults) the message that boys and girls naturally like different things. In reality, children are often naturally attracted to toys, clothes, hobbies, and other activities outside of their imaginary gender boxes. However, all of these cultural influences, from family to television to toy aisles, push children to play with the toys that are associated with their assigned sex and gender.

Even the language used to describe children often reinforces these gender roles. Children who are assigned as girls who enjoy toys and activities considered masculine are often called tomboys, emphasizing their masculinity, while those who prefer toys and activities considered feminine are often called girly girls. Children who are assigned as boys who prefer things considered feminine are often mocked and discouraged, while those who prefer things considered masculine are often praised for fulfilling male expectations. These

The courts are a powerful tool in the fight for equality for people of all gender identities.

Discrimination is often considered a legal issue, especially in the workplace. The highest court in the United States—the U.S. Supreme Court—has heard many cases throughout its history that have dealt with discrimination on the basis of sex and gender. One of the strongest champions of equal rights for people of all genders was Ruth Bader Ginsburg, who served on the Supreme Court from 1993 until her death in 2020. Even before her time as a Supreme Court justice, Ginsburg argued cases before the Supreme Court that made the world a fairer and more equal place, especially for women.

In 2020, Ginsburg was part of the majority who ruled in the case of *Bostock v. Clayton County* that workplace discrimination based on an individual's sexual orientation, gender identity, or identification as part of the LGBTQ+ community is prohibited by law. The court ruled 6–3 that this kind of discrimination constitutes discrimination on the basis of sex and therefore is not allowed under Title VII of the Civil Rights Act of 1964.

social effects create a lot of pressure to conform to gender roles, which can make it difficult for children to just be themselves. This is especially true for children who are intersex and transgender.

The Importance of Identity

Gender is an important part of a person's indentity. It's one of the many qualities that help a person know who they are. Gender can shape the way individuals see themselves, how they express themselves, and how they want others to see them. A person's internal sense of gender is their gender identity.

The relationship between social constructs and gender identities is complicated. Gender roles are social constructs, but a person's gender identity is personal and meaningful. According to writer Wiley Reading, "Gender identity is internal, deeply rooted, and a central part of many people's senses of self."[3]

Toxic Masculinity

Gender-based discrimination and stereotypical gender roles can have a negative impact on everyone. People who are assigned male at birth can face an immense amount of pressure from society—and often from their own family and friends—to fulfill unrealistic expectations of masculinity. Society sometimes glorifies hypermasculine traits, which creates a phenomenon that many people call "toxic masculinity." Writer Harris O'Malley explained:

Toxic masculinity is a narrow and repressive description of manhood, designating manhood as defined by violence, sex, status and aggression. It's the cultural ideal of manliness, where strength is everything while emotions are a weakness; where sex and brutality are yardsticks by which men are measured, while supposedly "feminine" traits— which can range from emotional vulnerability to simply not being hypersexual—are the means by which your status as "man" can be taken away.[1]

1. Harris O'Malley, "The Difference Between Toxic Masculinity and Being A Man," The Good Men Project, June 27, 2016, goodmenproject.com/featured-content/the-difference-between-toxic-masculinity-and-being-a-man-dg/.

Gender identity is deeper than society's messages and stereotypes about gender.

Most people have gender identities that match the sex and gender they were assigned at birth. The word used for this is "cisgender." Many people, though, have gender identities that are not the same as the sex and gender they were assigned at birth. "Transgender" is an umbrella term that includes all people who have a gender identity that is different from the sex and gender they were assigned. However, not everyone who has a gender identity that differs from their assigned sex and gender identifies as transgender. Likewise, not everyone who identifies as transgender agrees with this definition. Some people consider "transgender" to refer to only a specific identity and don't consider it an umbrella term. It's important to respect each person's terms and definitions. For the purposes of this book, "transgender" will be used as an umbrella term for those who have a gender identity that is different from the sex and gender they were assigned.

Gender identity is determined by the individual. It's unique to each person and cannot be assumed just by looking at someone.

The language used to describe gender identities has evolved over time. Many terms that were once commonly used are now considered offensive. Some of the terms that are common today may be considered outdated or offensive in the future. The following sections look at some of the terms that many people currently use to describe gender identities and the common definitions that accompany these terms. As gender identity is extremely personal, these terms can mean different things to different people. People need to respect the language individuals choose for themselves while also understanding that a term might be meaningful to one person and offensive to another. These terms should not be viewed as universal definitions that work for every person. In addition, under no circumstances should a person label someone else with a gender identity.

The Term "Transgender"

In addition to acting as an umbrella term, the word "transgender" can refer to a specific identity. Many people identify as transgender women or transgender men. The National Center for Transgender Equality (NCTE) offers the following definitions:

> "Transgender" is a broad term that can be used to describe people whose gender identity is different from the gender they were thought to be when they were born. "Trans" is shorthand for "transgender." (Note: Transgender is correctly used as an adjective, not a noun, thus "transgender people" is appropriate but "transgenders" is often viewed as disrespectful.) … Someone who lives as a woman today is called a transgender woman and should be referred to as "she" and "her." A transgender man lives as a man today and should be referred to as "he" and "him."[4]

Some transgender women sometimes refer to themselves as MTF, or "male-to-female," while some transgender men refer to themselves as FTM, or "female-to-male." This shorthand can be helpful for talking about issues specific to transitioning from living as a female to living as a male and vice versa. Not all transgender women and men use these terms, and many people see transitioning as more complex than these phrases acknowledge.

Nonbinary

The term "nonbinary" can also work in a number of different ways. To many, it's an umbrella term for genders outside the typical male/female binary. It's not necessarily the same as "trans." Not all people who identify as nonbinary also identify under the umbrella of transgender, and vice versa. It's completely up to each person to choose which term feels right for them.

Queer

The word "queer" has a history of derogatory use, but many people are reclaiming the term in different ways. In the 21st century, the term "genderqueer" is used by some people who feel their gender identity falls outside the traditional male/female binary or somewhere in between the two. While some definitions of genderqueer may sound very similar to some definitions of nonbinary, these words shouldn't be used interchangeably, unless an individual identifies with both terms.

A Fluid Option

Some people don't feel as though their gender is one unchanging thing. Many who feel this way use the term "gender-fluid" to describe their identity. In other cases, gender-fluid can be a description of a behavior. Not everyone who identifies as gender-fluid interprets this term the same way. As with all of these terms, it depends on the individual. For some, gender-fluidity means not subscribing to a specific label of masculine or feminine constantly but rather having the freedom to decide each day the gender identity they are most connected with. Their identity is expressed in behaviors, clothing choices, or interests and may blend stereotypically masculine and feminine roles. It's also important to keep in mind that not everyone will express themselves as masculine or feminine.

Bi-gender

Some people identify as two genders, such as female and male. Bi-gender people experience and express their identities in many

A person who doesn't ascribe to one particular gender but perhaps blends two or more may be called gender-fluid.

different ways. Some bi-gender people may express themselves as male one day and female the following day. The decision is up to them. Others will choose to align male and female aspects in other ways, such as through fashion or mannerisms.

Gender Neutral, Agender, or Neutrois

Some people don't identify as female or male. They instead see their gender identity as neutral. Other people consider themselves genderless and do not have a gender identity at all. In addition to genderless and gender neutral, "agender" and "neutrois" are two of the most common terms people use.

"Agender" can be an umbrella term or a specific identity by itself. People who identify as agender might not identify under terms such as transgender, nonbinary, genderqueer, or gender nonconforming (not conforming to stereotypical gender roles). To some, these terms imply identifying with a gender, which does not match how they feel about their own lack of gender. Others might be comfortable with one or more of such terms—it all depends on the person, and there is no right or wrong way to identify as agender.

Definitions of the term "neutrois" are often very similar to definitions of "agender," but the terms should not be used interchangeably. Neutrois.com explained, "Some neutrois [people] do feel completely genderless—that is, they have no gender, an absence of gender, or are null gendered. Others have an internal gender that is neither male, nor female, just neutral."[5] People who identify as neutrois may also identify as agender, nonbinary, or one or more other terms. Others may only identify as neutrois.

Cisgender People and Privilege

Cisgender people experience privilege because society has been designed for them. Countless aspects of daily life are divided into female and male categories: bathrooms, locker rooms, sports teams, clothing departments, hygiene products, organizations such as Girl Scouts and Boy Scouts, legal documents, and more. Cisgender people have a much easier time navigating these gender divides because no one questions their rights or choices. A cisgender girl can sign up for the girls' lacrosse team at her school without any trouble. A cisgender man can use the men's bathroom at work without worry. These seemingly small actions add up to an enormous amount of privilege that cisgender people can easily take for granted. In other words, society considers being cisgender the norm. Meanwhile, the transgender community has to fight for the same basic rights that cisgender people use without worry every day.

Cisgender privilege doesn't mean that cisgender people never face discrimination or difficulty. It simply means that they have an advantage in certain areas that the transgender community does not. Everyone's experiences are unique, and because there are many aspects to identity, every person experiences different combinations of privilege and difficulty.

A cisgender person doesn't have to feel bad about the areas in which they experience privilege, but they should look for

People who identify as the sex they were assigned at birth are considered cisgender, or cis.

Allies

Allies can be valuable confidants and supporters for LGBTQ+ people. Allies are people outside the community who uplift, fight for, and respect the LGBTQ+ community. They're integral support networks. According to the LGBTQ+ media organization GLAAD's annual acceptance report, in 2019, 63 percent of people ages 18 to 34 in the United States considered themselves allies. This percentage is a drop from years prior; however, it still points to a high level of acceptance for people in this generation.

It's extremely important for cisgender people to act as allies for the transgender community. They can use their positions of privilege to speak and act on behalf of the transgender community, which often struggles to have its concerns heard. According to a 2019 article for *Vox* titled "Here's What a Good LGBTQ Ally Looks Like," the best thing allies can do for their LGBTQ+ friends or family members is to support them in many ways—helping them financially if needed, taking part in protests, and by showing kindness, compassion, and awareness. This can be something as small as donating to an advocacy organization or making sure that transgender people's voices are heard in person and on social media.

Cisgender people should be careful not to single out transgender peers in their efforts to make spaces safer. This can lead their transgender peers to feel isolated and as if that part of their identity is all someone sees when they look at or talk to them. It's also important for cisgender people to remember not to make assumptions about the needs of their transgender peers. However, allies should always be ready to help should a need arise, and talking to their transgender peers—and really listening to them—is the best way to be ready.

ways to use that privilege to help others. This could be by joining in civil rights or equality movements or protests, getting involved in trans advocacy organizations, or standing up for someone experiencing discrimination.

What Is the Gender Spectrum?

If the gender binary is a social construct, but gender identity is a real and personal experience, then what exactly is gender? Even within the transgender community there are many different theories or ways of thinking about gender. Currently, one of the most dominant views is that gender is a spectrum.

Many people visualize the gender spectrum as a line with femininity at one end and masculinity at the other. Along this spectrum, there are many different gender identities ranging from extremely feminine to genderless, or neutral, to extremely masculine.

Some may prefer to visualize gender as a range of colors. Thinking in terms of colors may be more useful than a spectrum because it allows for all genders to be measured not by the amount they compare to the two most common gender identities and expressions, but simply by the way they exist. It also helps others think of gender in more ways than just a binary.

While visual tools, such as a color range or a Venn diagram with overlapping parts, can be helpful, it's important to realize that gender is much more complex and fluid than any diagram can represent. Thinking of gender as a spectrum works for many people, but it can also be problematic for others.

Diversity Is Good

Gender expression and gender identity come in many forms. Gender identity can change over time and be expressed in many different ways. People can encompass a range of genders or align with no gender at all. Societal expectations and ideas about gender have changed over time, and they are likely to continue to change. This is why it's important to try to think about gender identity and expression independent of society's stereotypes. Gender identity and expression are important aspects of the diversity of the human experience, and thinking beyond the binary helps us better understand ourselves and those around us.

Your Opinion Matters!

1. How do you express your gender identity? What are some ways you can encourage others to express theirs?

2. Why is gender identity important? How can you support people who identify in different ways than you do?

3. What are some examples of privilege in society today? Why might a white transgender person have different privileges than others in the transgender community? How can they help the wider community?

CHAPTER THREE

EMBRACING GENDER IDENTITY

Gender identity can be a tricky thing to navigate. So often, people hear messages about things being feminine and masculine, making it seem like they're the only options. It can be overwhelming or disheartening trying to understand gender identity alone. However, people don't have to explore this completely by themselves. There's a wider community out there waiting to help and embrace people for who they are.

A person's gender identity is closely related to gender expression. This is the way in which a person reveals their gender identity to society. Many people express themselves through their clothing, hairstyles, body language, or other physical attributes. Each person has a different way of expressing who they are, making us all unique.

Expressing Yourself

Although an internal sense of gender often shapes how people present themselves, gender identity and gender expression are two different things. Gender identity is how you feel on the inside, while gender expression is the way you express your gender outwardly. Sometimes a person's gender expression aligns with the gender binary, while other times it doesn't. For

◄ Many people express their gender outwardly.

instance, a person who identifies as a man can also choose to express themselves by wearing a dress, which is typically a piece of clothing worn by women.

Society has developed many stereotypes about gender expression. It categorizes certain aspects of physical appearance, types of clothing, and behaviors as feminine and others as masculine. However, human beings are more complex than this, and nearly everyone has a combination of both stereotypically feminine and masculine characteristics, behaviors, and interests.

Knowing

Many children quickly gain a sense of their gender identity. The American Academy of Pediatrics (AAP) stated, "By age four, most children have a stable sense of their gender identity. During this same time of life, children learn gender role behavior—that is, doing 'things that boys do' or 'things that girls do.'"[1] However, this isn't the case for everyone. Young children may explore different gender expression but later in life identify as cisgender. The reason for such a shift isn't known, but it could be either the result of a person hiding their true identity later in life or going through a phase of exploration in their youth.

Some transgender children don't go through a questioning or exploratory process, but simply know they identify with a gender other than the one they've been assigned. For example, activist Jordan Geddes shared, "Ever since I could remember, I'd always felt I'm a guy. From the age of 2, I would tell people I'm a boy. I even came up with a boy version of my birth name, and I would tell people I'm that. It was just never a question in my head."[2] Other transgender children take time to realize their identity. No matter how it unfolds, the discovery of gender identity is often a process. It can take people years to fully understand how they identify.

Many people begin to explore or discover their gender identities as teenagers. Puberty can sometimes influence how a person feels about their gender. That's because so many hormones and physiological processes are taking place inside the human body, challenging people and also changing them. These

Someone who is transgender could know this from a young age but not express it until later in life.

emotions and experiences, along with curiosity, may have teens contemplating their expression and identities closely. As a result, gender identity and gender expression can undergo intense study.

However, sometimes it's not until adulthood that someone accepts their gender identity or is able to find the right language to name it. A person may feel out of place in their body or in situations while maturing but not realize what they're going through until they're much older. Other people see discovering their gender identity as a process that began in childhood and took a long time.

Two Spirit

As gender is a social construct, cultures around the world all have their own variations of gender roles. Some societies recognize more than two genders. The concept of Two Spirit used by some Native Americans is one example. According to LGBTQ Health, "[The term] 'Two Spirit' refers to a person who identifies as having both a masculine and a feminine spirit."[1]

Definitions of Two Spirit may vary across Native communities or mean different things to different people. The Indian Health Service asserts, "Traditionally, Native American Two Spirit people were considered neither men nor women; they occupied a distinct, alternative gender status.'"[2] This terminology and the identity itself are unique to Native American cultures, and it is generally considered appropriation if non-Native American people use the Two Spirit term.

1. "Two-Spirit Community," LGBTQ Health, lgbtqhealth.ca/community/two-spirit.php (accessed March 17, 2020).

2. "Two Spirit," Indian Health Service, www.ihs.gov/lgbt/health/twospirit (accessed March 17, 2020).

Still others describe their gender identity as something they were born understanding.

There's no time frame on discovering and understanding gender identity. For many people, gender exploration is a fluid experience that changes throughout the course of their lifetime. No matter how young or how old a person is, their identity is valid and deserves respect.

Am I Enough?

From the moment a person begins questioning their gender identity, they may feel the need to figure out their gender identity and label it. It's common to struggle with different thoughts and feelings about identity and look to friends for help, and that's perfectly normal. It's important to remember that gender can be fluid.

Experimenting, exploring, and even uncertainty are all normal parts of experiencing gender.

However, this doesn't make it an easy process. Uncertainty can be difficult because someone may worry they're somehow "not trans enough" if they're not completely sure of their identity. Many transgender people share that they sometimes wonder if they're really trans. This sense of insecurity can come from society's lack of acceptance.

Feelings of not being "trans enough" can come from a variety of places. Unfortunately, sometimes the idea that there are certain standards of trans-ness come from within the transgender community itself.

When one person's definition of transgender is very different from another person's, it can lead some people to question who is "trans enough." Mia Violet offered this advice on dealing with disagreements in the transgender community:

> It's okay to disagree with other trans people. As long as what you're saying isn't harming anyone else, it's okay to disagree with concepts and terms related to being trans. I know people, friends even, who will disagree with things I've said here, but that's the point. Your gender identity is a very intimately personal part of you, if you disagree with someone's perception of what being transgender means to you then that's fine.[3]

The language we use to describe ourselves is always a deeply personal issue, and it's important to respect how other people choose to define themselves—and to advocate for your own sense of identity and the language used to describe it.

Confiding in Others

For many, coming out, or revealing your gender identity to family, friends, and a wider community, can be just as confusing and scary as the process of coming to terms with their own gender identity, but it's also an act of incredible bravery and self-love.

It can be extremely challenging for people to share their gender identity with their family, friends, and community. Blatant

It's not always easy coming out to family or friends.

discrimination against transgender people and society's typically strict enforcement of the gender binary can create a hostile environment for transgender people. They may not feel physically or emotionally safe expressing their gender identity, or they may choose to only share it with some people and not others.

Some transgender people experience negative reactions when they come out at home, at school, at work, or in other areas of their lives. Others find ready acceptance from family and friends. Often, people receive a range of positive and negative reactions from the different people they choose to come out to.

Finding acceptance from family and friends can be fulfilling and identity affirming, while dealing with rejection or negative reactions, especially from loved ones, can be extraordinarily challenging.

Coming out is different for everyone, and there's no one perfect way or time to do it. However, it's always important to feel physically and emotionally safe before you come out. Planning ahead can be crucial to ensure safety. Questions people often consider before coming out to others include: Will I be safe in my home if I do this? Will I be accepted by my family and friends? Could I lose my job? How could different laws protect me if I did? While these questions can be difficult to think about, there are resources to help transgender people find safe, healthy ways to come out. Organizations promoting LGBTQ+ activities, social groups, and civil rights actions are excellent places to get informed or to give aid.

If someone shares their gender identity with you, it's extremely important not to out them, or share their gender identity without their consent. It's possible that the person's physical and emotional well-being are at stake. GLAAD's "Tips for Allies for Transgender People" page explained:

> A transgender person's gender history is personal information and it is up to them to share it with others. Do not casually share this information, speculate, or gossip about a person you know or think is transgender. Not only is this an invasion of privacy, it also can have negative consequences in a world that is very intolerant of gender diversity. Transgender people can lose jobs, housing, friends, or even their lives when other people find out about their gender history.[4]

As some transgender people are only out to certain people, they may present themselves differently in different situations. For example, a teenage transgender girl might express femininity and go by "she" and "her" pronouns and a name she has chosen for herself around friends, but express masculinity and go by "he" and "his" pronouns and a given name at home. Transgender teens with parents who are prejudiced against the transgender community may not feel safe coming out to their family. Their physical and emotional safety could be at risk if they are outed by someone else.

Coming out is generally an ongoing process. People have to decide whether or not to come out to the people already in their life, and then make the decision again with each new relationship they form. The attitudes of loved ones can also change over time, for better or worse. For example, sometimes transgender people find their friends and family support one aspect of their gender identity but react negatively to another.

LGBTQ+ people who are accepted by family and friends often feel better about themselves.

It's important to show others respect and love if they come out to you, and to know that you deserve to be shown love and support if you come out to another person. While coming out isn't always a scary or negative experience, it takes lots of courage and planning to do so.

Your Opinion Matters!

1. What are some examples of ways people can outwardly express their gender identity?

2. Why might some people acknowledge their gender identity sooner than others?

3. What are some good examples of supportive words and behaviors you can use if someone comes out to you or wants to talk to you about their gender identity and expression?

CHAPTER FOUR

THE IMPORTANCE OF LANGUAGE

Much of our communication with others revolves around language. It's one of the things that brings us together, helps us express our emotions and thoughts, and makes us unique. However, language is largely a social construct and therefore open to change. Within the transgender community, language is very important.

The Use of Pronouns

The way words are used and the order they are used in matter. Pronouns, or words that take the place of nouns, are especially important to people in the transgender community. In some languages, there are masculine, feminine, and gender-neutral pronouns. In English, for example, "he" and "his" are masculine pronouns, "she" and "hers" are feminine pronouns, and "they" or "theirs" are gender-neutral pronouns. It's important to know what pronouns people use and to apply them in conversations with others. This shows respect and kindness.

Why Pronouns Matter

Many transgender people are not comfortable with the pronouns associated with their assigned sex and instead identify

◀ Knowing the pronouns people use and then using those pronouns can make places such as schools and offices feel safer and more inclusive.

Changing It Up Is OK

Grammar may seem like a code of unbreakable rules, but it's actually changing and growing with the culture all the time. Some of these changes happen so subtly that people don't even notice them, and many people who notice don't care as long as the meaning of a word or sentence is clear. For instance, in the past, the word "stream" was used to define a flow of liquid or gas. After technology advanced to the point where people could use the internet in their homes, another meaning was added to the word "stream": a flow of digital data.

These changes are important to note because people who use "they" instead of gendered pronouns may be corrected by people who dislike that they're breaking a grammar rule. In English, "they" used to be known as a plural pronoun, but many dictionaries have changed to allow the singular usage. Also, English-speaking people have been using the word "they" as a singular pronoun for centuries. Even famous writers such as Jane Austen and William Shakespeare did this!

with a different set of pronouns that they feel better suits their gender identity. These are often described as "preferred pronouns." While many people are comfortable with this term, it's better to simply say "pronouns." The word "preferred" makes it sound as though there are other acceptable options. However, you are the only person who gets to decide your pronouns.

If someone isn't comfortable with the pronouns associated with their assigned sex, finding pronouns that they feel good about can be an identity-affirming process. To find the right pronoun, people can try switching between pronouns to see which works best for them, decide to use a mix of pronouns depending on situations or comfort, or create their own pronouns.

People deserve to have their identity respected and to be described using language they are comfortable with. Using the pronouns that someone is comfortable with shows them that their gender identity is respected and also that they are respected as a person.

Neutrality

Anyone can choose to go by "she" and "her," "he" and "his," or a combination of both, even if they don't identify as strictly female or male. However, many people are not satisfied with these two options because they each carry stereotypes and ideas that are rooted in the gender binary. In other cases, people might identify with femininity and masculinity, but these polarized pronouns still don't feel right.

Gender-neutral pronouns are developing to fill these gaps in gender language. As of 2020, the most popular gender-neutral choice in English is the singular form of "they." This word describes a person without ascribing a gender. For example, "Robin always plays their bass after school. They're a very talented musician." "They" and "their" have become an empowering option for transgender, nonbinary, and gender nonconforming people who don't want to identify themselves with feminine or masculine words.

Showing Respect

One of the most important steps in respecting someone's pronouns is to avoid making assumptions. Making assumptions about a person's pronouns is similar to making assumptions about that person's gender identity. Assumptions about a stranger's gender identity are based on the stereotypes of femininity and masculinity resulting from the gender binary. When someone assumes a person's gender identity from their appearance, the gender binary and its narrow concepts about femininity and masculinity are being supported. Instead of assuming what someone's pronouns are, ask them which pronouns they use.

Today, many people are choosing to display their pronouns outright. This is especially true on social media. On the platform Twitter, for instance, more and more people are displaying their pronouns in the brief description about them in their profile or in their username. Choosing to display pronouns in the digital era helps answer questions others might have and fosters respect for all.

Pronouns help people speak to and about each other. The most common pronouns are "she/her," "he/him," and "they/them."

Making It Normal

Conversations about pronouns can be awkward, especially when people are meeting for the first time. However, it's important to have these kinds of talks with others to better understand them and show respect to them.

In group settings, such as the first day of class, having everyone introduce themselves and tell their pronouns can be a positive way to ensure everyone feels comfortable and safe. Writer West Anderson describes this as a "pronoun round." They wrote:

> This practice takes the pressure off trans people to announce their pronouns to the rest of the group and makes asking for and sharing pronouns a normal part of introductions. If a space is made for everyone to share their pronouns before discussion begins, it

can avoid misgendering a group member unknowingly or putting a trans person on the spot to announce their pronouns to a group alone. It works to create spaces in which we don't assume someone's pronouns from their appearance.[1]

Anderson explained, "The purpose of a pronoun round is to normalize the sharing of pronouns so that everyone can be correctly referred to without 'othering' trans people."[2]

Misgendering

Misgendering, or referring to someone by a gender other than their gender identity, can take many forms. Any situation in which a person is labeled as a gender with which they don't identify as is an act of misgendering. Pronouns are one of the most common ways people are misgendered. This can happen in any setting—at school, at work, out in public, or even at home. In any situation, intentional misgendering is harmful and unacceptable. Above all, misgendering someone is an act of disrespect. Pronouns, names, and language are important tools for validating identity. No one has the right to use those tools in a way that makes someone uncomfortable.

However, accidents do happen, and sometimes misgendering is unintentional. If that happens, the person who misgendered someone should be gently corrected. They should apologize and then make an effort to improve in other conversations going forward. The Lesbian, Gay, Bisexual, and Transgender Resource Center of the University of Milwaukee stated:

A lot of the time it can be tempting to go on and on about how bad you feel that you messed up or how hard it is for you to get it right. But please, don't! It is inappropriate and makes the person who was misgendered feel awkward and responsible for comforting you, which is absolutely not their job.[3]

If a person is misgendered in any capacity, they have a right to be upset. They deserve to feel safe and respected.

On the other hand, continual misgendering is very different from accidental misgendering. If someone constantly

Language can sometimes be used as a kind of weapon to hurt others.

misgenders someone, they're making a deliberate decision not to respect that person or their wishes. Such actions, in turn, can lead to others misgendering that person as well.

A New Name

Transgender people often choose a new name for themselves. The name they were called before is often called a dead name, as it no longer applies to them. They may choose a new name

Correcting Gendered Language in Everyday Use

Society is full of unnecessarily gendered language and phrases. Teachers address their classes as "boys and girls," waiters call their customers "sir" or "miss," friends call each other "bro," "man," or "dude." While this language seems harmless, it supports the gender binary and erases transgender and nonbinary identities. It also creates a culture where people are easily misgendered. Writer Adrian Ballou explained that when a person uses gendered language, "You run the risk of misgendering someone, using sexism [a commonly used word for gender-based discrimination, often toward women] to justify your gender judgments, enacting sexism by interacting with someone based on their (a)gender identity, and generally being rude—because it's rude to assume that you know someone else better than they themselves do."[1]

One alternative to gendered language when addressing a stranger is to simply tell them your name and ask for theirs. Saying, "excuse me," to get someone's attention is another alternative to calling someone "sir" or "miss." These simple gestures can help transgender people feel comfortable and accepted.

1. Adrian Ballou, "7 Tired Phrases That Marginalize Trans People—And What to Use Instead," *Everyday Feminism*, February 3, 2015, everydayfeminism. com/2015/02/phrases-marginalize-trans-people/.

that reflects their gender identity or a gender-neutral name. Some people decide to legally change their name, while others simply go by a new name in their daily lives without going through the legal process. Still others don't change their name at all. As with all experiences, choosing a new name—or choosing to keep a given name—is different for each person. As the article "How Transgender People Choose Their Names" points out, "Many transgender people choose new names to go by before, during, or after their transition to their true gender, whether it's because their dead name … is too masculine or feminine, too binary, or just doesn't fit them anymore."[4] No matter the reason, choosing a new name can be an empowering part of embracing gender identity—and it's not limited to first names. Last names can change too.

For some people, asking for family members' opinions can be very meaningful in the name-changing process. This brings people together while also ensuring people close to the person changing their name are kept informed and journey with them through the entire transitioning period. However, some people might not want

Finding a new name can mean doing a lot of research, but it's all worth it in the end.

to choose a family name or even involve their family in the decision process. It all depends on the person, the relationships they have, and their unique situation.

Sometimes, finding a new name without any associations feels right. For others, a collaborative approach feels more natural. Others may consult baby books or choose their name from an online persona they invented, a game they played, or a piece of media that means something to them.

There is no right or wrong way for a person to find a name they love. Inspiration can come from anywhere. Finding a name with meaning, with family history, or that simply feels right can be a powerful experience.

Adjusting to a New Name

Getting used to a new name can be difficult, and this is completely normal. Sometimes people need to try out multiple names before they find the right one. Even when someone finds a new name they like, adjusting might still be challenging.

A name change is an adjustment to the person changing their name as well as to the people who knew them prior to the change. Ideally, all will work together to understand the change and put new words to use. It may seem strange at first to use different pronouns or a different name for someone. However, the more people use someone's chosen name and pronouns, the easier it will be. People who have changed their name have often found it be a liberating and fulfilling experience in the long run and a way to live life authentically and fully.

Not Alone

Once someone chooses a new name, the aftermath can vary. Claiming your true self through the adoption of different or new pronouns and a name change is a big step. However, not everyone that a person knew before their transition—including coworkers, friends, or even close family—will understand or support them. This can be incredibly hard on a transgender person, making

A new name can help a transgender person break out of their old life and embrace their true self.

them question their own decisions and even their own purpose in the world.

Sometimes, accepting your true self can lead to a lack of acceptance from others—and even to the loss of a family or home. Transgender young adults may become homeless after rejection by a family member or guardian or the loss of a job after transitioning. Thankfully, several organizations today help LGBTQ+ people in need. Groups such as the Trevor Project, True Colors United, and the National Coalition for the Homeless work hard to assist and welcome LGBTQ+ youth who are struggling. Each group provides youth with different resources, such as a safe place to stay, counseling, or training to help them through difficult times.

Your Opinion Matters!

1. Do you understand why language is important? How can you make sure you're using the correct language with people you care about?

2. What are some reasons an individual might be hesitant to come out to everyone they know? How could you help someone make a transition to a new life easier?

3. Why do names matter? Do you feel your name reflects your identity?

CHANGES AND TRANSFORMATIONS

People who know their authentic self is different from the sex and gender they were assigned may choose to go through physical changes as well as changes concerning language. People who change their physical appearance to best align with their identity go through a process called transitioning. To transition means to change, and transitioning can mean many things—from changing one's outward appearance and fashion to undergoing medical procedures or receiving voice therapy to change speech patterns or inflection.

Gender Dysphoria

Transitioning is often a part of working through gender dysphoria. The American Psychiatric Association (APA) explained:

> *Gender dysphoria involves a conflict between a person's physical or assigned gender and the gender with which he/she/they identify. People with gender dysphoria may be very uncomfortable with the gender they were assigned, sometimes described as being uncomfortable with their body (particularly developments during puberty) or being uncomfortable with the expected roles of their assigned gender.*[1]

Gender expression can change as a person gains a deeper understanding of their gender identity and how they want to show that to the world.

Many transgender people experience some form of gender dysphoria. Dysphoria can take many forms, and it affects everyone differently. Some transgender people do not experience dysphoria at all. Rather, a person can be uncomfortable with different parts of their assigned sex, rather than the entirety of their assigned sex.

Gender dysphoria used to be called "gender identity disorder" by the APA. Referring to this experience as a "disorder" was deeply offensive to the transgender community because it implied there was something wrong or unnatural about being transgender. In 2013, the APA changed this term to "gender dysphoria." In doing so, the APA acknowledged the need for a more respectful term and that this change was an important step toward eliminating the stigma surrounding the transgender community. This change was included in the fifth edition of the APA's *Diagnostic and Statistical Manual of Mental Disorders*, or *DSM-5*, a comprehensive volume of psychological terms. However, many object to classifying gender dysphoria in the *DSM-5*. That's because they consider gender dysphoria a state of being rather than a mental condition. Others argue that inclusion in this medical text allows for better access to medical provisions such as hormone therapy and surgeries, which otherwise might not be granted.

Society often reduces the transgender experience to "being born in the wrong body." For many transgender people, this idea is stereotypical, inaccurate, or offensive. In reality, gender dysphoria feels different for each person, and it should never be oversimplified or dismissed.

Certain sensations, events, or interactions can trigger feelings of dysphoria in a person. The causes of gender dysphoria are different for everyone. Some people experience gender dysphoria during particular tasks. It can also be caused by external forces such as family and friends.

Navigating Gender Dysphoria

As gender dysphoria affects everyone differently, each person experiencing it will probably find their own ways of handling the symptoms. In any case, it's important to practice self-care. This means making emotional and physical needs a priority and giving yourself permission to do things that make you feel good.

Finding ways to assert individual identity can help some people handle gender dysphoria. Clothing, hairstyles, makeup, and other forms of gender expression can be empowering and helpful for alleviating gender dysphoria. Some people find body modifications, like tattoos or piercings, help them feel more in control over their body as well.

Embracing other aspects of one's identity, such as one's culture, can sometimes help with gender dysphoria too. Gender expression and roles are vastly different from culture to culture. Connecting with a cultural identity can give someone a better sense of self and purpose and give people the strength to continue with their journey.

Professional help from a psychologist, counselor, or therapist who's qualified to assist transgender patients may also be incredibly helpful in handling gender dysphoria and other difficulties. It's important for transgender people seeking mental health treatment to find a professional who is accepting of the transgender community and with whom they personally feel comfortable talking. Cities and towns may have lists of transgender-focused counselors and therapists. Support groups are also popular ways to connect with the rest of the LGBTQ+ community and engage in discussions about the transition process.

Changing Appearances

Gender dysphoria can take the form of someone being anxious or depressed because they wish they had certain body parts, wish they didn't have certain body parts, or have a combination of these feelings. Many people find that altering their body's appearance with nonmedical tools can help with gender dysphoria. Packing, tucking, padding, and binding are all common practices that allow people to take control over their appearance. However, not everyone who alters their appearance suffers from gender dysphoria, and using these tools doesn't always mean that gender dysphoria will go away.

Packing is wearing a prosthetic, or nonflesh, penis. Packing can help people look and feel more masculine, which may help with gender dysphoria.

Tucking is the process by which a person conceals their natural penis and other reproductive parts. Tucking can help create a more feminine appearance.

Padding is using undergarments or other material to create the illusion of larger breasts, hips, or buttocks. Padding can help create a traditionally feminine figure.

Binding is a process in which a person wears tight clothing, bandages, or compression pieces to flatten the chest region. This creates a smooth, masculine appearance. Wearing sports bras and several layers of clothing can be helpful alternatives to binding.

It's important that, no matter which technique one might choose, they follow appropriate steps and complete these techniques carefully. For example, a person who binds should take off the bindings before going to sleep. LGBTQ+ organizations provide helpful information about these processes and safety measures related to them.

The Transitioning Process

Transitioning is the process a transgender person undergoes when they begin to live by their gender identity instead of by the sex and gender they were assigned at birth. Choosing to transition, or not to transition, is a deeply personal process. According to GLAAD:

> Transition can include some or all of the following personal, medical, and legal steps: telling one's family, friends, and coworkers; using a different name and new pronouns; dressing differently; changing one's name and/or sex on legal documents; hormone therapy; and possibly (though not always) one or more types of surgery. The exact steps involved in transition vary from person to person.[2]

Some people choose to only transition socially. They may also only openly transition in certain areas of their life, or around certain people, where they feel safe and accepted. People who choose to medically transition have many options on how to do so. There is

A person who's transitioning may be able to change their name and sex on different documents, including driver's licenses, passports, and Social Security cards.

not one path to medically transitioning. Not all transgender people choose to transition either socially or medically; it's completely up to the individual.

Surgical Steps

Medical transitioning involves making physical changes to one's body to better reflect one's gender identity. This can include hormone therapy, one or more surgeries, or a combination of the two. Hormone therapy uses hormones to help develop secondary sex characteristics that align with a person's gender identity and minimize the secondary sex characteristics that don't align with their gender

Steps of Social Transitioning

Here are some of the steps a person may choose to take when socially transitioning:

- Changing their name, either legally or informally
- Using different pronouns
- Changing their gender expression through fashion sense, hairstyling, makeup, or physical details such as facial hair or piercings and tattoos
- Explaining their decisions to family and friends
- Coming out at school or at work (This often involves speaking with administration at school or human resources at work.)
- Changing their gender marker on forms of identification, such as a driver's license or school I.D.
- Using bathrooms in school, at work, or in public that suit their gender identity
- Participating in clubs, organizations, and activities that suit their gender identity—for example, joining the women's soccer team at their school or singing in a men's choir
- Moving to a college dorm that suits their gender identity (if their college separates dorms by gender)

These are just some of the ways people can transition socially. Each person will make amendments to their social life as they see appropriate, and some processes may take more time or be more difficult than others.

identity. Surgical options alter a person's anatomy. They include breast removal or reduction or breast insertion or enhancement (also called "top surgery"), genital surgery (also called "bottom surgery"), and removing reproductive organs (such as through a hysterectomy or orchiectomy). This is also known as gender-affirming surgery.

According to the American Society of Plastic Surgeons, more than 9,500 gender-affirming surgeries were conducted in the United States in 2018. That was an increase from around 8,300 surgeries in 2017. This indicates a growing trend, and experts predict

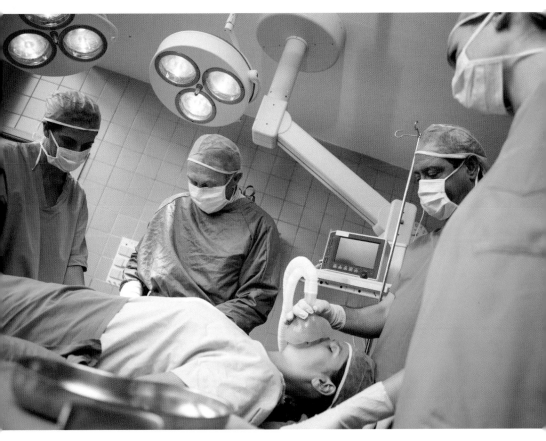

Surgery is not uncommon for transgender individuals; however, not everyone who is transgender decides to have surgery.

this number will continue increasing. However, not all transgender people choose surgery. In fact, many elect not to have surgeries, either due to cost, the risks associated with surgery, or having no desire to change their body through surgery. People choosing to pursue hormone therapy and gender-affirming surgery may undergo a process of trial and error before they're happy with the results of their treatment.

Managing Hormones

Estrogen is used in hormone therapy for people who want to develop secondary sex characteristics that society considers feminine.

Through this kind of therapy, people will typically develop breasts, experience reduced muscle mass and body hair, change sweat and odor patterns, and possibly reverse hair loss.

As of 2020, 17-beta (or 17-B) estradiol is the most common class of estrogen used in this type of hormone therapy. It's bioidentical to the hormone that is naturally created in human ovaries. This helps people develop "feminine" secondary sex characteristics. People taking estrogen also often use testosterone blockers call antiandrogens, which work to minimize "masculine" secondary sex characteristics. Using antiandrogens allows people to take lower doses of estrogen.

People who want to develop "masculine" secondary sex characteristics and suppress "feminine" secondary sex characteristics can

It can be helpful for transgender people to discuss all parts of their transition process with a therapist or other mental health professional.

take hormone therapy involving testosterone. All of the testosterone preparations used in hormone therapy are bioidentical to the testosterone naturally produced inside human testicles. People who use this type of therapy will typically develop facial hair and increased body hair, experience vocal changes, gain muscle mass, change sweat and odor patterns, and possibly develop receding hairlines or baldness.

In both estrogen and testosterone hormone therapy, results happen gradually over time and differ from person to person. Mood swings are a common side effect of both types of therapy. Estrogen therapy can potentially lead to increased risk for blood clots, high blood pressure, or estrogen-related cancers. These risks can be monitored through blood tests and routine breast cancer screenings. Testosterone therapy can potentially cause high cholesterol, blood clots, weight gain, and diabetes. With either type of therapy, consistent health screenings are helpful for avoiding these risks.

Affording Health Care

Paying for and managing health care and medical transitioning can be extremely difficult for transgender individuals. However, in the United States, federal and state laws prohibit discrimination against a person based on their sexual orientation or gender identity. While some states have been trying to change that, as of 2020 "it is illegal discrimination for [a] health insurance plan to refuse to cover medically necessary transition-related care."[3] Still, many health insurance policies and programs don't cover all expenses dealing with surgery or other elements of transitioning. In 2017, a survey of LGBTQ+ people conducted by the Center for American Progress (CAP) reported that 29 percent of participants were refused medical care because of their gender identity.

The truth is, medically transitioning is a necessity for many transgender individuals. According to Lambda Legal, a leading LGBTQ+ advocacy group, "Courts have … found that psychotherapy alone [to treat gender dysphoria] can be insufficient treatment … for some people, gender-affirming surgery [and hormone therapy] may be the only effective treatment."[4]

Military Service and Transgender People

In many conflicts involving the United States, people of all backgrounds have raced to help their country. Up until 2016, transgender people couldn't serve openly in the military. However, there were some people who did so secretly. The military ban was lifted after much struggle in 2016. Soldiers who were transgender finally could join the military and live and work openly. However, that changed during Donald Trump's presidency. According to the Human Rights Campaign, "On July 26, 2017, President Trump posted a series of tweets in the early morning hours stating that '[t]he United States Government will not accept or allow transgender individuals to serve in any capacity in the U.S. Military.'"[1]

The military ban was officially announced in March 2018. It said that no openly transgender person could join the military, but those who were already serving could continue to do so. Several courts issued injunctions, or orders that blocked this order, but the Supreme Court lifted those injunctions. However, the election of Joe Biden as U.S. president in 2020 led to the reversal of this policy. On January 25, 2021, Biden signed an executive order that overturned the Trump administration's ban on transgender soldiers in the U.S. military.

1. "Transgender Military Service," HRC.org, www.hrc.org/resources/transgender-military-service (accessed March 19, 2020).

Despite calls from some conservative lawmakers to make drastic changes to the rights of transgender youth and adults across the country, many organizations continue to push for equal health care for the transgender community. There are laws in place to protect transgender individuals' rights to medical access. The Affordable Care Act prohibits discrimination based on gender identity and makes it illegal to refuse to cover someone based on their gender identity or to refuse to cover the costs of transition treatment. The Health Insurance Portability and Accountability Act (HIPAA) also protects the privacy of transgender individuals' medical records, including their transition status. Still, much work needs to be done to ensure transgender people have access to the health care they need.

Mental and Emotional Health

Choosing to medically transition is an extremely personal decision, and each person's experience is unique. In addition to side effects and bodily changes, medically transitioning can be an incredibly difficult emotional journey. Other personal health concerns such as mental illness can have a large impact on a person's experience of medically transitioning.

In the United States, transgender youth endure great amounts of stress, which is sometimes the result of homelessness or joblessness

There's a growing population of LGBTQ+ youth in America today. It's important for them to have access to mental health care if they need it. This can allow them to live happier, healthier lives.

after coming out, side effects of hormone therapy, or discrimination and bullying. Many deal with harmful or suicidal thoughts. According to a 2019 study by the Trevor Project, 35 percent of transgender youth attempted suicide between 2018 and 2019. That same study revealed that about half the number of transgender youth polled had experienced moments of depression. Mental health is an increasing concern today, as people recognize its importance to living a full and happy life. Seeking guidance from professional counselors who are well educated in transgender issues can be a crucial part of the transition process.

Aftermath of Surgery

The permanence of surgeries can also be extremely intimidating. Some people may worry they'll regret their decision, while others feel confident in their choice even before surgery.

Choosing to medically transition or not to medically transition may be a long process. Ultimately, it's a personal choice, and there's no right or wrong decision. Choosing either course of action doesn't at all impact whether or not a person is transgender, as one's gender identity doesn't rely on going through a medical transition.

Handling Stereotypes

Society often expects transgender people to express their gender in hyperfeminine or hypermasculine ways that fit neatly into the gender binary. This image of transgender people is harmful because it oversimplifies the complex relationship between gender identity and expression. Everyone expresses themselves differently and to different degrees. Fitting into a stereotype is not the goal of exploring and understanding your gender identity.

Transgender people often face more pressure to conform to the gender binary's stereotypes than cisgender people. That's because society sometimes expects a person in transition to want to be exactly like the stereotypical gender they're transitioning toward and not see gender as being fluid or complex. However, that's not true. There are varying degrees of gender identity and gender expression. Finding which combination of traits works for you is part of everyone's life story, regardless of how you identify.

Your Opinion Matters!

1. What are some ways people can be supportive allies to someone going through the medical transition process?
2. How do you feel about the various policies and revisions surrounding transgender members of the U.S. military?
3. Why is mental health care an especially important part of the transition process?

DIFFICULTIES, TRIUMPHS, AND CHAMPIONS

In the 21st century, society has made progress in welcoming and accepting the transgender community. The majority of Americans know someone who is LGBTQ+, and more programs, support groups, and health-care workers are providing essential social, emotional, and medical outlets for those individuals. However, discrimination still exists, and many transgender people continue to be targeted.

Pride

In the United States, some leaders and state lawmakers have tried to limit transgender rights or erase them completely. However, there are also advocates and organizations constantly working for the LGBTQ+ community and winning. Yearly Pride parades and events during the month of June, as well as LGBT History Month in October, also offer important times for people to come together and support the LGBTQ+ community.

June marks the start of Pride month. This is a time when many parades and other LGBTQ+ activities take place. June was selected for Pride month because it was in June 1969 that the Stonewall riots occurred. Members of the LGBTQ+ community and allies take part in Pride events in various cities, hoping to

Pride parades and other events happen around the world. They're ways for the LGBTQ+ community and allies to come together to celebrate their victories and hope for a more equal future.

join in solidarity with others and educate the public about LGBTQ+ rights and people. Pride celebrations aren't limited to the United States. Communities around the world sponsor their own Pride parades, workshops, and conferences as well.

In the United States, October was designated LGBT History Month in 1994. People join together to remember the struggles the LGBTQ+ community has faced and the hard work key figures have put in to securing crucial rights for LGBTQ+ people today. Importantly, it offers people the chance to connect with the LGBTQ+ community in meaningful and impactful ways and through dialogue, marches, vigils, and volunteer opportunities.

Strength and Struggle

Some of the most important voices for the transgender community include the American Civil Liberties Union (ACLU), the National Center for Transgender Equality, and the Trevor Project. Many citizens and politicians are also pushing for laws that will continue to protect the transgender community and ensure its rights are maintained.

However, other changes are also needed. In addition to changing laws, society needs to eradicate its many forms of transphobia. From media outlets to conversations among friends, some parts of society still promote transphobic language and negative attitudes toward the transgender community.

Many in the transgender community have faced difficult and frightening treatment by others. This ranges from bullying and harassment to conversion therapy. More people are openly talking about the problems faced by the transgender community, but more understanding is needed in order to eliminate these practices.

What Is Conversion Therapy?

Conversion therapy involves "counselors" attempting to change a person's sexuality or gender identity, which can lead to devastating mental and emotional effects on LGBTQ+ people. Conversion therapy is a practice dismissed by the majority of the medical and psychological community as unnecessary, unethical, and abusive. Some parents of LGBTQ+ youth force their children to undergo conversion therapy to try to change their sexuality to heterosexual or their gender identity to cisgender.

According to the 2019 LGBT Youth Mental Health Survey by the Trevor Project, "67 percent of youth polled said someone attempted to convince them to change their sexual orientation or gender identity."[1] Minors (those under the age of 18) often cannot escape this abusive situation, and many suffer intense feelings of depression or thoughts of suicide as a result. LGBTQ+ and human rights organizations continue to fight on their behalf to ban conversion therapy altogether.

Young people questioning their gender identity might be subjected to conversion therapy by their parents, who believe that being transgender (or any other part of the LGBTQ+ community) is a problem to be "fixed."

As of late 2020, conversion therapy is banned in 20 states, including New York, California, Illinois, New Jersey, Oregon, Vermont, and Utah, as well as the District of Columbia, and more states are introducing similar legislation—including ones that previously passed laws protecting the practice of conversion therapy, such as Oklahoma. In states where conversion therapy is banned, licensed mental health providers can't offer conversion therapy to minors.

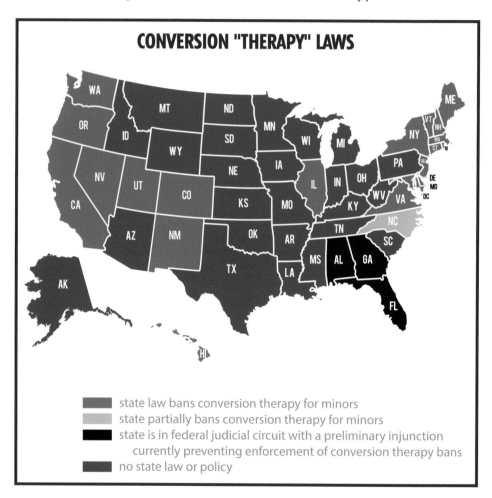

CONVERSION "THERAPY" LAWS

- state law bans conversion therapy for minors
- state partially bans conversion therapy for minors
- state is in federal judicial circuit with a preliminary injunction currently preventing enforcement of conversion therapy bans
- no state law or policy

This map from the Movement Advancement Project shows the laws and policies concerning conversion therapy in each U.S. state. Many LGBTQ+ organizations put therapy in quotes because it's not a real form of therapy or mental health care.

Protecting Rights

Each state and city is responsible for passing and enforcing its own laws concerning LGBTQ+ rights. Federal laws encompassing LGBTQ+ rights include Title VII of the Civil Rights Act of 1964 and Title IX of the Education Amendments of 1972.

Title VII of the Civil Rights Act protects against discrimination in public places. Title IX, enacted in 1972, states, "No person in the United States shall, on the basis of sex, be excluded from participation in, be denied the benefits of, or be subjected to discrimination under any education program or activity receiving Federal financial assistance."[1] It was originally put in place to prevent against discrimination in education. However, many people today also apply it universally. It's facing scrutiny, though, especially as it relates to how universities handle sexual assault cases.

In addition to these laws, President Joe Biden has issued executive orders—directives from the president that act as laws—aimed at protecting the rights of the LGBTQ+ community. One such executive order was his lifting of the ban on transgender people serving in the military. Another executive order signed by Biden prevents workplace discrimination on the basis of sexual orientation or gender identity.

In order to fully protect LGBTQ+ citizens, many allies and advocates think clearer federal laws should be passed. However, there are challenges posed by different religious groups and politicians, and new anti-LGBTQ+ bills are being proposed in states each year.

1. "Title IX and Sex Discrimination," U.S. Department of Education, www2.ed.gov/about/offices/list/ocr/docs/tix_dis.html (accessed March 20, 2020).

Mental Impact

There's a misconception that simply being transgender causes mental health issues, but this is not at all the case. The immense pressure and discrimination that society exerts upon transgender people can negatively impact their mental health. The National Alliance on Mental Illness (NAMI) recommends, "Early intervention, comprehensive treatment, and family support are key to helping LGBTQ people live well with a mental health condition. But many people in this community struggle in silence—and face worse health outcomes as a result."[2] The Trevor Project's National Survey on Youth Mental Health reports, "39 percent of LGBT youth seriously considered attempting suicide in the past 12 months, with more than half of transgender and non-binary youth having seriously considered."[3] However, not all mental stressors relate to one's gender identity. It's also completely possible for transgender people to experience mental health issues that are unrelated to their gender identity.

Mental health professionals who are educated on transgender issues can help individuals in many ways, such as helping them with:

- Exploring gender identity and learning self-acceptance
- Coping with gender dysphoria
- Coming out and socially transitioning
- Deciding whether or not to pursue medical transitioning and discussing medical transitioning options
- General mental health issues unrelated to their gender identity

Research suggests that accepting environments can have a positive effect on transgender people's mental health. That's because if people are accepted for who they are, especially by people they trust and love, they're likely to feel more valued in society. The Human Rights Campaign reports that more than 90 percent of LGBTQ+ youth are out to their close support networks. Having as many of those network connections validate and support someone can make a big difference for a person's well-being.

Residential and Financial Struggle

According to 2019 research by the National Center for Biotechnology Information, between 20 and 40 percent of the homelessness population is made up of LGBTQ+ people, including LGBTQ+ youth. True Colors United reported, "It's estimated … that 40% of youth experiencing homelessness are LGBTQ."[4]

Homelessness can happen for a number of reasons, and there are services doing what they can to help those in need.

Many organizations, like True Colors United, seek to ensure equal housing for the LGBTQ+ community, lessen the rates of homelessness among members of the LGBTQ+ community, and eliminate discriminatory shelter policies. The U.S. Department of Housing and Urban Development has also enacted policies that protect transgender renters and homebuyers from discrimination based on their gender identities, but more work needs to be done to end transphobic practices.

Harmful Acts

The transgender community continues to experience many forms of violence, particularly against transgender women of color. According to a 2019 study by the Williams Institute, "LGBT people are victims of person-based (rather than property-based) violence at higher rates than victims of religiously or racially motivated crimes."[5] This includes domestic abuse and hate-induced violence such as rape or murder. In 2018, the FBI reported a jump in hate crimes committed against members of the LGBTQ+ community. About 19 percent of the hate crimes reported that year targeted LGBTQ+ people. This

We Remember

In 1999, Gwendolyn Ann Smith founded the Transgender Day of Remembrance (TDOR) in honor of Rita Hester, a transgender woman who was killed in 1998. TDOR is held annually on November 20. On this day, vigils takes place to remember those lost to anti-transgender violence and raise awareness of crimes against the transgender community. Transgender advocacy groups and LGBTQ+ organizations across the country hold vigils in parks, places of worship, and other public places. Vigils generally include a reading of the list of names of the transgender people who were killed in acts of anti-transgender violence that year.

The aftermath of the Pulse nightclub terrorist attack included scenes such as this, including flowers, messages, and signs of solidarity.

was a 16-year high, according to reports, and a major indication that more needs to be done to protect LGBTQ+ citizens.

One of the most tragic incidents of violence toward the LGBTQ+ community happened on June 12, 2016, when the Pulse nightclub in Orlando, Florida, was the scene of a domestic terrorism attack. The assailant, Omar Mateen, entered the club and opened fire, killing 49 people and injuring 53 before he himself was killed by police. This horrific event jarred the world and scarred the LGBTQ+ community. In its aftermath, thousands of messages and gifts of hope and love flooded the Orlando area. There's still much work to be done to protect all members of the LGBTQ+ community in all aspects of life, but support for this community is often shown in powerful ways.

Government Response

Under President Barack Obama from 2009 to 2017, much progress was made toward including the LGBTQ+ community in all facets of society, most notably when the U.S. Supreme Court legalized same-sex marriage in 2015. In regard to health care, the administration lifted restrictions on members of same-sex couples visiting each other in hospitals. It likewise pushed for more anti-discrimination legislation as it pertained to workplaces and businesses such as restaurants, stores, and shelters.

However, as the Trump administration took power in 2017, many government actions and considerations in place under Obama began to change. For example, soon after taking office, President Trump's administration began taking down White House websites concerning LGBTQ+ rights, especially in regard to health care and health data collection. This alienation of the LGBTQ+ community dismantled many steps of progress that had been made by the Obama administration and seemed to send a message to the LGBTQ+ community that its members were not welcome or appreciated. The Trump administration also promoted measures that protected religious businesses from serving LGBTQ+ clients and repealed rules that allowed transgender students to use the restroom that matched their gender identity.

These changes were stressful and disheartening for many, especially after so many gains had been made. However, many state legislatures around the United States continued to uphold and introduce laws that protected LGBTQ+ people. Organizations such as Lambda Legal and the Human Rights Campaign also continued to advocate for inclusive environments and better treatment for all Americans, especially those most vulnerable to discrimination.

Furthermore, the election of Joe Biden as U.S. president in 2020 was seen as a positive sign for the LGBTQ+ community and especially for transgender people. Biden has spoken publicly about the need to support the transgender community and to make its members feel welcomed, protected, and respected. His support for the LGBTQ+ community and his commitment to inclusivity was evident from the first day of his administration, when he signed an

One issue affecting some states today is how to accommodate the presence of transgender people in public restrooms. Some businesses have opted for unisex restrooms rather than gender-specific ones to clear up any questions.

executive order banning workplace discrimination on the basis of sexual orientation or gender identity. Biden also nominated the first openly transgender person for a Cabinet position—Dr. Rachel Levine, who was his choice for assistant health secretary.

Anti-Transgender Bills

Despite the hope a Biden presidency brought, conservative politicians have continued to push for anti-transgender laws that discriminate against the transgender community. One issue that entered the public eye in 2015 was the use of public restrooms in schools. Some state lawmakers introduced legislation that prohibited transgender people from using the restroom that aligned with their gender identity. This caused great controversy and debate across America, angering many.

People continue to introduce more laws targeting the transgender community. In 2020, for example, two state bills targeting the transgender community were introduced and then passed in Idaho. One bill stated that transgender people can't alter their birth certificates. Another said transgender women and girls couldn't participate on female sports teams. This treatment by lawmakers is deeply hurtful and worrying for many LGBTQ+ people and allies. It not only dismisses their gender identity, but it also works to further alienate them from society.

Businesses and LGBTQ+ Customers

In the midst of the discriminatory bathroom legislation issue, some companies came out in support of the LGBTQ+ community. One of the first was Target, which publicly stated that transgender employees and shoppers were welcome to use whichever bathrooms and dressing rooms they felt comfortable in. In response, a conservative Christian group called the American Family Association started a boycott in protest of Target's inclusive policies. Rather than backing down, Target committed $20 million to creating gender-neutral bathrooms in all its stores. Other companies followed suit, and even more continue to be advocates for their LGBTQ+ workers. Some of the most LGBTQ+ friendly organizations, according to the Human Rights Campaign's 2020 Corporate Equality Index, include Amazon, Airbnb, 3M, Apple, Microsoft, Mattel, and Kohl's. These companies ranked high in terms of nondiscriminatory practices, gender-inclusive health care and benefits, and employee diversity and satisfaction.

Other companies lean anti-LGBTQ+, strongly opposing service to anyone who identifies as such and challenges a business owner's religious or moral beliefs. An example of this appeared in 2017, when a bakery in Lakewood, Colorado, refused service to a same-sex couple, claiming religious reasons were behind their decision. This treatment sparked a debate across the United States, one that still continues today. Can a business reject customers based on its owners' religious or moral standings? In this case, a court ruled in the couple's favor. However, other instances of discrimination haven't resulted in such outcomes. Negative or alienating reactions toward the LGBTQ+ community harm a person's self-worth but also risk a business's credibility and future.

Media Presence

From the earliest childhood experiences and throughout a person's life, many of the messages people receive about gender come from the media. A crucial element to eliminating transphobia and discrimination against the transgender community is accurate, respectful representation of transgender individuals in the media. Without representation, the transgender community continues to be treated as "other" by the majority of society. Allowing transgender voices in the media helps address discrimination, inspires positive change, and normalizes and embraces the transgender community as equal members of society.

Today, more TV shows are starting to introduce transgender characters. More and more, these roles are being played by transgender actors, too, which is good news for the acting community and their audience. Examples of hit shows with trans or nonbinary characters include *Orange is the New Black*, *Pose*, *Euphoria*, and *Grey's Anatomy*. Actors such as Laverne Cox, Mj Rodriguez, Hunter Schafer, and Alex Blue Davis are taking center stage by portraying characters with impactful personalities and similar gender identities to their own. By placing actors from the LGBTQ+ community in fulfilling roles, such shows will not only bring recognition of the community to the forefront but also pave the way for more acceptance of LGBTQ+ people in society as a whole.

Community Heroes

There are many LGBTQ+ people changing the world today, especially when it comes to perceptions of gender and issues relating to gender identity. The following list is only a sample of people in the larger community who are changing lives and hearts. Each person offers a unique experience and voice in support of the LGBTQ+ community.

Laverne Cox played Sophia Burset on Netflix's *Orange Is the New Black* and has appeared in a number of different roles since then. She is the first trans woman of color to play a leading role on a mainstream scripted television show and the first openly transgender person to ever be nominated for an Emmy Award. Cox is also renowned for her eloquent, moving speeches about transgender issues, sexism, and racism.

Janet Mock is a writer, director, and TV producer. She's perhaps best known as one of the producers, writers, and directors of the TV show *Pose*, which is about life for LGBTQ+ people, especially trans women of color, in the 1980s and 1990s in New York City. In 2018, she directed the episode "Love Is the Message." This made her the first trans woman of color to direct an episode of television. She later signed a production deal with Netflix, making her the first trans woman of color to reach this creative milestone.

Jonathan Van Ness is best known as a member of the "Fab 5," five LGBTQ+ individuals who make over the appearances and lives of many on their hit Netflix show *Queer Eye*. He is known for his motivating speeches, gender-fluid style, positive attitude, and hair and skin expertise. He identifies as nonbinary/gender non-conforming.

Jazz Jennings is a transgender woman and a lead LGBTQ+ activist. Originally a YouTube star, she's one of the youngest people to have their transition documented for the public. Today, she has her own TV show on The Learning

Jazz Jennings has worked hard to affirm her gender identity through various medical procedures and gender expression. She is an inspiration for many.

Channel (TLC), *I am Jazz*, and in 2016 her autobiography, *Being Jazz: My Life as a (Transgender) Teen*, was published.

Lady Gaga is a hit musician and actress, best known for her music as well as her roles in the 2018 remake of *A Star Is Born* and the TV show *American Horror Story*. Her songs, such as "Born This Way," have become anthems for the LGBTQ+ community. Lady Gaga has also been a leading advocate for the LGBTQ+ community, participating in marches, mentioning the community in acceptance speeches, and incorporating transgender individuals into music videos and film projects.

Making Change

Although much progress has been made to create a more open and accepting society, there's still much that needs to be done to create a world where people of all gender identities feel accepted, respected, and safe. It's never too early to start doing your part to make this world a reality. If you want to be an ally, you can go to rallies or marches and write to government leaders on behalf of the LGBTQ+ community. However, you can also be an ally simply by supporting LGBTQ+ people you know and doing small but important things such as using proper pronouns.

If you identify as a member of the LGBTQ+ community or have questions about your gender identity or any other topic, the most important thing to know is that you're not alone. From supportive family members and teachers or coaches to school friends and online communities, there are people you can lean on as you discover more about yourself and grow more comfortable with your identity and how you want to express it. If you want to share your identity with the world, that's great! However, you don't have to rush yourself. Everyone has their own story, and they can share it in their own time when they're ready. Being kind to and accepting of others is important, but it's just as important to be kind to and accepting of yourself.

Your Opinion Matters!

1. Think of some new nationwide laws that could help the LGBTQ+ community. Why should they be adopted by the federal government? How could you help them get recognized by lawmakers?

2. What are some positive examples of portrayals of LGBTQ+ people (especially trans people) in the media? Why is it so important for the media to represent different gender identities?

3. How can you help make the world more inclusive for people of all gender identities?

GETTING INVOLVED

The following are some suggestions for taking what you've just read and applying that information to your everyday life.

- Stand up for those who need help or are being bullied or harassed.

- Think about your gender identity, and talk openly about gender identity and expression with people in your life.

- If you identify as a gender other than the sex you were assigned at birth, share your story and your truth with others if you feel comfortable. However, remember that you don't have to share anything you don't feel comfortable sharing and you shouldn't rush the process of self-discovery and self-acceptance.

- If you're struggling with issues related to your gender identity, talk to a trusted adult.

- Be kind and understanding if a friend or family member comes out to you.

- Educate others on the importance of acceptance in society.

- Read articles and books by LGBTQ+ authors, and watch movies and TV shows that represent LGBTQ+ people and issues in a positive way.

- Volunteer at a homeless shelter that accommodates LGBTQ+ youth.

- Donate to LGBTQ+ organizations.

- Join your school's LGBTQ+ group or form your own.

- Promote Pride month in June.

NOTES

Introduction: A Place in History

1. Susan Miller, "The Young Are Regarded As the Most Tolerant Generation. That's Why Results of This LGBTQ Survey Are 'Alarming'," *USA Today*, June 24, 2019, www.usatoday.com/story/news/nation/2019/06/24/lgbtq-acceptance-millennials-decline-glaad-survey/1503758001.

Chapter One: Understanding Sex

1. "Physical Development in Boys: What to Expect," The American Academy of Pediatrics, November 21, 2015, www.healthychildren.org/English/ages-stages/gradeschool/puberty/Pages/Physical-Development-Boys-What-to-Expect.aspx.

2. "Answers to Your Questions about Individuals with Intersex Conditions," American Psychological Association, www.apa.org/topics/lgbt/intersex.pdf (accessed March 16, 2020).

3. "I Want to be Like Nature Made Me," Human Rights Watch, July 25, 2017, www.hrw.org/report/2017/07/25/i-want-be-nature-made-me/medically-unnecessary-surgeries-intersex-children-us#.

4. "Understanding Gender," Gender Spectrum, www.genderspectrum.org/quick-links/understanding-gender/.

Chapter Two: Understanding Gender

1. "Sexual Violence Is Preventable," CDC, www.cdc.gov/injury/features/sexual-violence/index.html (accessed March 16, 2020).

2. "The Simple Truth About the Gender Pay Gap," www.aauw.org/files/2016/02/Simple-Truth-Update-2019_v2-002.pdf (accessed March 16, 2020).

3. JR Thorpe, "11 Ways To Be A Trans* Ally, According To Transgender People Themselves," Bustle, www.bustle.com/articles/76762-11-ways-to-be-a-trans-ally-according-to-transgender-people-themselves.

4. "Understanding Transgender People: The Basics," National Center for Transgender Equality, July 9, 2016, transequality.org/issues/resources/understanding-transgender-people-the-basics.

5. "What Is Neutrois?" Neutrois.com, neutrois.com/what-is-neutrois/ (accessed March 17, 2020).

Chapter Three: Embracing Gender Identity

1. "Gender Identity Development in Children," The American Academy of Pediatrics, November 21, 2015, www.healthychildren.org/English/ages-stages/gradeschool/Pages/Gender-Identity-and-Gender-Confusion-In-Children.aspx.

2. Quoted in German Lopez, "9 Transgender People Talk about When They Knew, Coming Out, and Finding Love," *Vox*, April 23, 2015, www.vox.com/a/transgender-stories.

3. Mia Violet, "Yes, You're 'Trans Enough' to Be Transgender," *Huffington Post*, March 6, 2016, www.huffingtonpost.com/mia-violet/yes-youre-trans-enough-to_b_9318754.html.

4. GLAAD, "Tips for Allies of Trasgender People," www.glaad.org/transgender/allies (accessed March 17, 2020).

Chapter Four: The Importance of Language

1. West Anderson, "Pronoun Round Etiquette: How to Create Spaces That Are More Inclusive," The Body Is Not An Apology, October 22, 2016, thebodyisnotanapology.com/magazine/pronoun-round-etiquette/.

2. West Anderson, "Pronoun Round Etiquette: How to Create Spaces That Are More Inclusive."

3. "What If I Make a Mistake?" University of Wisconsin-Milwaukee LGBT Resource Center, uwm.edu/lgbtrc/qa_faqs/what-if-i-make-a-mistake/ (accessed March 18, 2020).

4. Adryan Corcione, "How Transgender People Choose Their Names," *TeenVogue*, August 2, 2018, www.teenvogue.com/story/how-transgender-people-choose-their-names.

Chapter Five: Changes and Transformations

1. "Gender Dysphoria," American Psychiatric Association, February 2016, www.psychiatry.org/patients-families/gender-dysphoria.

2. "GLAAD Media Reference Guide—Transgender," GLAAD, www.glaad.org/reference/transgender (accessed March 18, 2020).

3. "What Are My Rights in Insurance Coverage?" National Center for Transgender Equality, transequality.org/know-your-rights/health-care (accessed March 18, 2020).

4. "FAQ: Equal Access to Health Care," Lambda Legal, www.lambdalegal.org/know-your-rights/article/trans-related-care-faq (accessed March 18, 2020).

Chapter Six: Difficulties, Triumphs, and Champions

1. "National Survey on LGBTQ Youth mental Health," The Trevor Project, www.thetrevorproject.org/survey-2019/?section=Conversion-Therapy-Change-Attempts (accessed March 20, 2020).

2. "LGBTQ," The National Alliance on Mental Illness, www.nami.org/Find-Support/LGBTQ (accessed March 20, 2020).

3. "National Survey on LGBTQ Youth mental Health," The Trevor Project.

4. "Our Issue," True Colors United, truecolorsunited.org/our-issue (accessed March 20, 2020).

5. "New Study on Gun Violence Against LGBT People," The Williams Institute, April 30, 2019, williamsinstitute.law.ucla.edu/press/gun-violence-sgm-press-release.

FOR MORE INFORMATION

Books: Nonfiction

Jennings, Jazz. *Being Jazz: My Life as a (Transgender) Teen*. New York, NY: Ember, 2016.

McKenna, Miles. *Out!: How to Be Your Authentic Self*. New York, NY: Amulet Books, 2020.

Reimer, Matthew, and Leighton Brown. *We Are Everywhere: Protest, Power, and Pride in the History of Queer Liberation*. New York, NY: Ten Speed Press, 2019.

Books: Fiction

Jaigirdar, Adiba. *The Henna Wars*. Salem, MA: Page Street Kids, 2020.

Panetta, Kevin. *Bloom*. New York, NY: First Second, 2019.

Smyth, Ciara. *The Falling in Love Montage*. New York, NY: HarperTeen, 2020.

Stamper, Phil. *The Gravity of Us*. New York, NY: Bloomsbury YA, 2020.

Websites

GLAAD

www.glaad.org

GLAAD is a leading advocate, media outlet, and voice for the LGBTQ+ community in the United States and around the world.

National Center for Transgender Equality

transequality.org

The National Center for Transgender Equality is a lead advocate for the LGBTQ+ community, working closely with other agencies to ensure rights and protections for all.

Transgender Law Center

transgenderlawcenter.org

The Transgender Law Center is the largest trans-led organization advocating for trans and LGBTQ+ rights in the United States.

Organizations

InterACT Advocates for Intersex Youth

365 Boston Post Road, Suite 163

Sudbury, MA 01776

interactadvocates.org

twitter.com/interact_adv

InterACT Advocates for Intersex Youth is an organization dedicated to raising awareness of intersex issues, empowering young intersex activists, and advocating for laws and policies that protect intersex youth.

The National Suicide Prevention Lifeline

Phone: (800) 273-8255 (800-273-TALK)

suicidepreventionlifeline.org

This service provides free, confidential crisis support for anyone who is considering suicide for any reason. A live chat is also available through the website.

Trans Lifeline

101 Broadway #311

Oakland, CA 94607

Phone: (877) 330-6366

www.translifeline.org

twitter.com/TransLifeline

This nonprofit organization began in 2014 by members of the transgender community. Its focus remains on the transgender community. The goal of the organization is to help transgender people who are considering harming themselves, but it welcomes anyone who feels overwhelmed to call.

The Trevor Project

P.O. Box 69232

West Hollywood, CA 90069

Phone (Lifeline): (866) 488-7386

Text: (202) 304-1200

www.instagram.com/trevorproject/

www.thetrevorproject.org

twitter.com/trevorproject

www.youtube.com/thetrevorproject

The Trevor Project is a nonprofit organization that provides resources for LGBTQ+ people from ages 13 to 24 who are considering self-harm or suicide. The Lifeline is available 24 hours a day, 7 days a week for people who need to talk to a crisis intervention counselor immediately.

True Colors United

311 West 43rd Street, 12th floor

New York, NY 10036

www.instagram.com/truecolorsunited/

truecolorsunited.org

twitter.com/truecolorsunite

www.youtube.com/c/TrueColorsUnited

Started in 2008 by musician and LGBTQ+ advocate Cyndi Lauper, today True Colors United is one of the leading voices for homeless LGBTQ+ youth in the United States. The organization offers training and resources for homeless shelters, teaching essential techniques and methods for navigating LGBTQ+ homelessness in communities.

INDEX

A

advertisements, 25–26
Affordable Care Act, 72
agender, 34–35
allies, 37, 47, 77, 81, 87, 90
American Academy of Pediatrics
  (AAP), 17–18, 42
American Association of University
  Women, 26
American Civil Liberties Union
  (ACLU), 78
American Psychiatric Association,
  63
American Psychological
  Association, 18
American Society of Plastic
  Surgeons, 68
antiandrogens, 70

B

Ballou, Adrian, 57
Band of Lovers, 6
Biden, Joe, 72, 81, 85–86
bi-gender, 33–34
binding, 65–66
Bostock v. Clayton County, 29
bullying, 74, 78

C

Center for American Progress
  (CAP), 71
Centers for Disease Control and
  Prevention (CDC), 26

chromosomes, 16, 18, 20
cisgender, 25, 30, 35–37, 42, 74,
  79
Civil Rights Act, 29, 81
civil rights movement, 10
color range, 38
conversion therapy, 78–80
Cox, Laverne, 88–89

D

dead name, 56, 58
*Diagnostic and Statistical Manual
  of Mental Disorders, 5th Edition
  (DSM-5)*, 64
discrimination, 5, 25–26, 29–30,
  36–37, 45, 57, 71–72, 74, 77,
  81, 83, 85–88

E

Equal Pay Act, 26–27
estrogen, 15, 18, 69–71

F

"feminine" toys, 28

G

Geddes, Jordan, 42
gender-affirming surgery, 68–69,
  71
gender binary, 13, 15, 19, 21, 38,
  41, 46, 53, 57, 74

P

packing, 65–66
padding, 65–66
Paycheck Fairness Act, 27
Pride month, 77
pronouns, 47, 51–55, 59, 66, 68, 90
protests, 8, 37, 87
puberty, 15–18, 42, 63
public restrooms, 86
Pulse nightclub, 84

R

rallies, 90
Reading, Wiley, 29

S

secondary sex characteristics, 15, 18, 67, 69–70
stereotypes, 21, 24–25, 30, 38, 42, 53, 74
Stonewall riots, 8, 77
social media, 25, 37, 53
surgery, 19, 66, 68–69, 71, 74

T

Target, 87

testosterone, 15, 18, 70–71
Title VII, 29, 81
Title IX, 81
toxic masculinity, 30
transgender, 5, 8, 10–11, 25, 29–33, 35–38, 42, 45–48, 51, 53, 55–57, 59–60, 64–67, 69, 71–74, 77–78, 81–83, 85–90
Transgender Day of Remembrance (TDOR), 83
transition, 11, 32, 57–60, 63, 65–68, 71–74, 82, 89
Trevor Project, 61, 74, 78–79, 82
True Colors United, 61, 82–83
tucking, 65–66
Two Spirit, 44

U

U.S. Department of Housing and Urban Development, 83
U.S. Supreme Court, 29, 72, 85

V

Van Ness, Jonathan, 89

W

Walker, Mary Edwards, 7

PHOTO CREDITS

ABOUT THE AUTHOR

Anika Abraham is a writer from Buffalo, New York. She loves writing about and reading books and articles on history, psychology, animals, personal stories, and current events. She lives with her partner and two cats.